The
ABSENT ATOM

William Reveley

ISBN 979-8-88832-883-5 (paperback)
ISBN 979-8-88832-884-2 (digital)

Christian Faith Publishing
832 Park Avenue
Meadville, PA 16335
www.christianfaithpublishing.com

The ideas and opinions here are solely those of the author and do not imply or reflect views of any federal agency, other organizations, or individuals.

Figures by Alphagraphics U.S. 641

Printed in the United States of America

Whatever may be the characteristic or curvature of the space, and however it may vary from point to point or remain constant, an element of space—that is an infinitely small part of it—is plane or Euclidean.
—Albert Einstein

Preface

There have been three basic assumptions in the intuitive continuous field model described here. Primarily, it is understood that any charged particle, including the orbital electron, is unaccelerated if it does not radiate electromagnetic energy. Secondly, every single atom in the universe has a surrounding positive gravitational field that has its source in a negative or hyperbolic distortion of the space-time manifold located within the atom itself. Finally, that these two guiding principles dictate the structure of the atom.

The only rational source of that imposed negative curvature is the coupled matter wave that we see in the atom's orbital electron field. The continuous field model of the atom developed here will evolve completely logically and will show a collapsed field around a stable invariant coupled matter wave of the orbital electron. That electron will have a reversed time coordinate (e.g., a clock that is running fast rather than slow). These conditions will be shown to allow the orbital electron to move locally along a geodesic, a local straight line. Included in the narrative are elementary diagrams illustrating basic principles of geometry primarily directed toward the average reader with some scientific background. Likewise, the narrative is as elementary as possible for the same reasons.

In the discussion, new concepts that may particularly interest the reader, such as a fast-running clock and its logical origin, will have surfaced. Also, a distance will be seen as short or long depending on the perspective of the viewer.

Lastly, a discussion of the surprising things that follow from the model. The most basic is that the fundamental gravitational force in the universe is reactive in the sense of repelling, not "attractive," a push instead of a pull. This leads to the conclusion that the existence of black holes is problematic, considering that *total gravitational collapse* is impossible. The so-called dark energy would disappear in this hyperbolic universe where galaxies naturally accelerate away from each other.

So you, the reader, jump in, activate and animate your imagination and enter a new universe.

The Absent Atom

To the average man over the long sweep of history, the smallest element of himself and his world was not something to which he gave much thought. Only those with a fascination for natural things let their imagination focus on what that final result of seemingly endless divide of a physical object would be. There must be a stopping point, the one last indestructible bit.

It was Democritus in the fifth century BC who gave the atom, that final infinitesimal bit, its name, from the term *atomos*, meaning "divisible." His teacher, Leucippus, was to have the great intellectual leap. At that time, the wise men, the erudite, had considered things that have different physical manifestations—things resistant to the touch, such as rocks, grass, and liquids—as separate elements. Leucippus had observed that water on a cold night had transmuted to ice, a hard substance decidedly different from the liquid it had come from. Ice and water were generally seen as two different elements. Leucippus saw it differently. He, with his student Democritus, proposed that changes in matter resulted in the arrangements of atoms. In that view, ice and water were composed of the same atoms, both the same element, but ice had a more rigid grouping. It was not a change in the element of water itself but a completely *local* change that was reflected in its different external appearance. He visualized matter as being composed of atoms separated by empty space. His atoms were solid and unchangeable, differing in size and shape. Leucippus's observations were the earliest records of the idea of local action. Things that appeared different were only different because their most basic elements had different arrangements.

In many ways, if not most, the theme here is of local action. Here is a logic road map of that theme:

(a) The universe is filled with gravitating objects: stars, planets, and moons. They are surrounded with gravitational fields. If you remove the atoms one by one from any of them, their gravitational field would become weaker and weaker until you would be left with a last single atom. It would have a very weak but real gravitational field.

(b) It would be obvious then that the gravitational field of a gravitating object was due to the cumulative effect of all the individual gravitational fields of its compositional atoms. Perhaps simplistic but it is a statement that *the source of the field lies within the single atom.*

(c) The field around the single atom would be a *relaxation* field, the space-time manifold, since it gets weaker as you move away from the source. It is also a positive field geometrically since its radii of curvature have the same mathematical sign.

(d) Inside the atom, we look for the mechanism that distorts the space-time manifold in a negative or hyperbolic way. In other words, the radii noted in *c* above would have different signs. Why negative? This is the character of multidistorted manifolds to be seen later.

(e) The mechanism for a negative space-time field distortion has at least two possible sources: the nucleus and the surrounding electron field. Nature is not so devious as to use here two separate mechanisms to produce the distortion. And that distortion would be in both locations, not just one. The nucleus is such a high-energy place it has been difficult to learn much about it. The electron field is a different case. We search there for the distorting mechanism.

(f) We have to look at only one place for that mechanism. It is the coupled matter wave of the stable orbital electron. In the atom's electron field, there is no other anomalistic location that would be a candidate. The enigma of the coupled matter wave is a hundred years old. In the 1920s, every scientist knew that when any charged particle was accelerated, it radiated electromagnetic energy (see fig. 1). Yet when in the hydrogen-atom electron-capture process, an electron curves into the potential field of the central proton. It loses energy through radiation because it is being accelerated. That is until *the matter wave that accompanies the electron becomes in phase with itself*, and it stabilizes into orbit there. The enigma is why there is no radiation in a phased orbit but there is radiation elsewhere. The mechanism for energy gain or loss when an orbital electron changes levels is always acceleration. "What is the difference between a coupled wave and an uncoupled one?" is the hundred-year-old question that was continually sidestepped.

The Absent Atom is an intuitive logic chain that tries, among other things, to resolve the expressed coupled-matter-wave enigma and will lead to the conclusion that the laws of mechanics and geometry around a coupled matter wave will *force a reversal of the time coordinate there.*

Simple Curvature

The logical sequence of how we get to the prior conclusion will require some background, largely developed with the more general reader in mind who has an interest in science.

Generally, at a point on a symmetrical curved surface, we have a radius of curvature. It points toward the center of the best circular segment we can construct at the point. In fig. 2, we can see two curves point in the same direction and have the same sign. This is a positive surface. On another surface (fig. 3), we see radii pointing in opposite directions. In this situation, the radii have different signs, one negative and one positive. This is a negative surface. Using a mathematical description, we can say,

$$C = k / (r_1\, r_2)$$

(where C is the curvature, k a proportionality constant,
and r_1 and r_2 are the appropriate radii)

There are other more rigorous mathematical descriptions of formal curvature, but this simpler one will work for us. In application, we look at two different surfaces—one positive and one negative. We look at the method in fig. 2 to illustrate a positive surface using the surface of a spheroid or, more familiarly, the surface of a football. We have constructed a vertical or normal from the point of the surface we wish to evaluate. We use that vertical as the axis of a paddle wheel or two planes that are set at right angles to each other. If we rotate the wheel until the two curves are generated, where the planes cut the surface of the spheroid have radii that reach a maximum or minimum at the test point we are evaluating, we then use these two radii. The maximum or minimum can be just one or both (as on a sphere, for example). The two radii we obtain there will be put in the curvature equation to give us the curvature at our test point.

The second figure (fig. 3) is a saddle shape which will represent a negative point. Using the rotating plane process, we will find that the two curves have their radii in *opposite* directions. This says one is positive, the other, negative. If we substitute these two values into our curvature equation, the resulting *C* value is negative. So we know that our test point on this saddle or *hyperbolic* surface is negative.

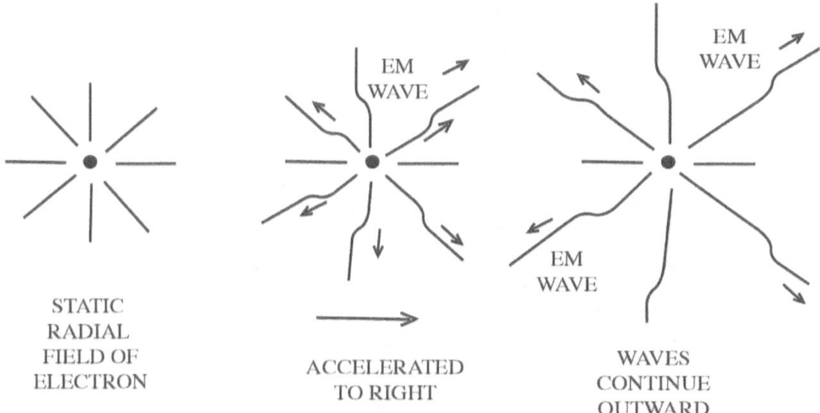

Fig. 1. As an electron is accelerated to the right as above, the kinks in the radial field lines move outward at the speed of light. The kinks are electromagnetic waves. Under angular acceleration, as in our electron, the only key difference from the above linear model is that the electron's field lines are displaced by rotation, producing the characteristic "kink" or EM wave that you see in the figure above.

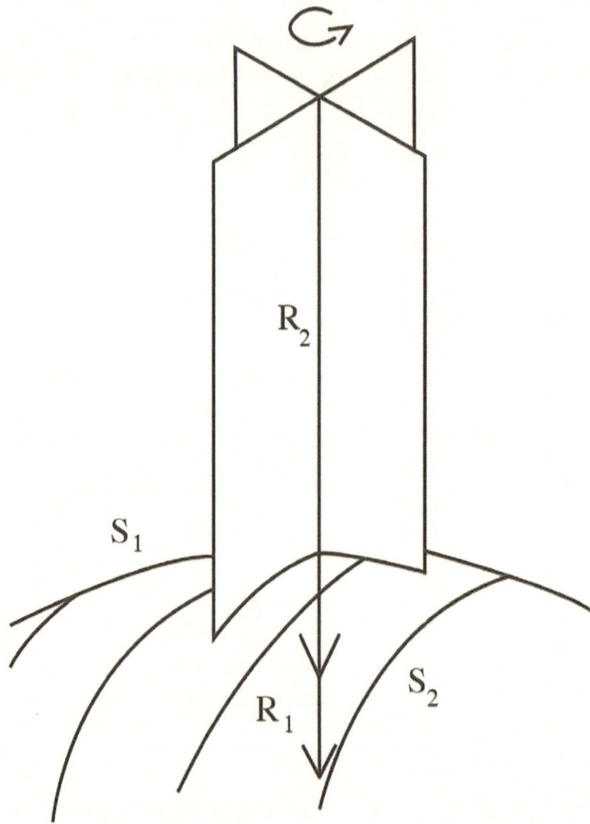

Fig. 2. In developing the curvature of a positive surface, the two right angle planes cut the surface in two arc segments. Note that the two characteristic radii both point in the same direction.

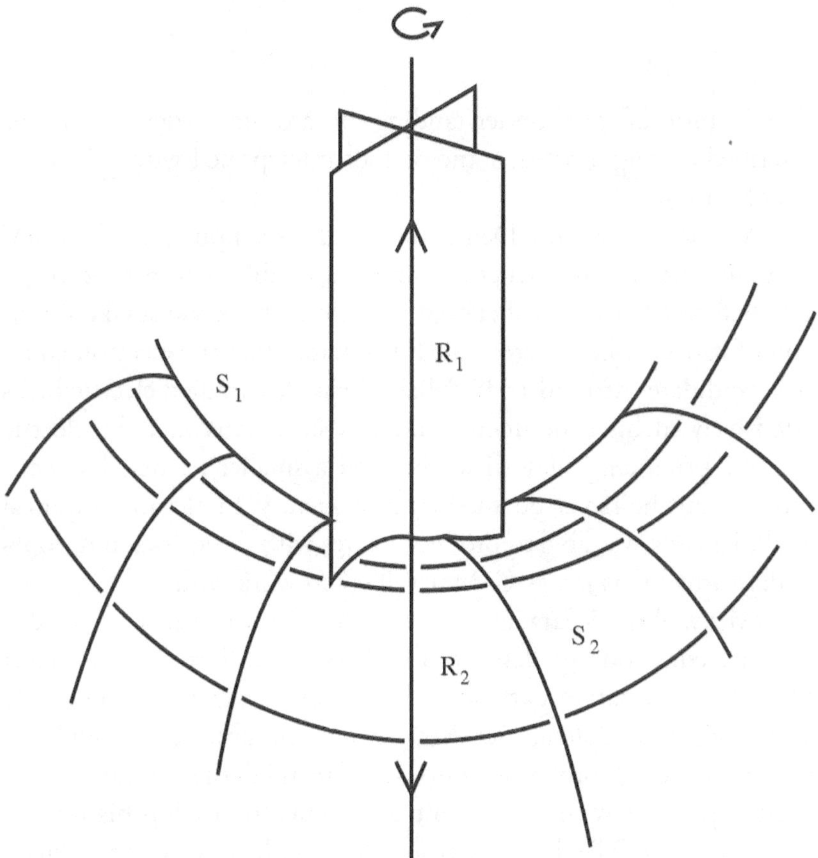

Fig. 3. The above shows the curvature of a saddle-shaped negative surface. Note that our right-angle planes cut the surfaces such that the characteristic radii point in opposite directions.

History and Background

The history of our understanding of atomic structure can be described as long, unclear static periods interspersed with brief periods of clarity.

We can start with Democritus and Leucippus and their single-point atom—indestructible and indivisible—in fifth century BC. Before 1897, it was believed that atoms were the smallest division of matter. There were some hints before that the electron could be a candidate. Around 1839, Michael Faraday studied electric fields extensively in his experiments and was suspicious that the electric currents producing these fields implied a smaller particle-like constituent, but he never pursued it subsequently. In elegant empirical work, Faraday was able to produce curves with intensities and slopes or derivatives that James C. Maxwell could work with.

Maxwell used Faraday's work as the basis of twenty vector differential equations to describe Faraday's fields, but even he never alluded to a separate particle to help explain electric currents. He knew, however, that an accelerating current produced a building field that would propagate outward. He used the Faraday group of his equations with subsequent operations to develop his famous wave equation. The Faraday group dealt with how changing magnetic fields produced changing electric fields. Maxwell, among other works, used the equation to calculate the average velocity of a propagating wave between two arbitrary points, A and B, and compared it to then extant measurements of the velocity of light. They matched almost exactly.

Maxwell's work was done between 1861 and 1866. Afterward, he was able to say and write, "Light is an electromagnetic disturbance propagated through the field according to electromagnetic laws."

His equations would be useful in feeding into theoretical calculations related to the atom after the turn of the century. My personal experience with eighteen of Maxwell's equations involved government contractors using them to shape the fields for xenon electric thrusters useful in north–south satellite-station keeping and other applications.

In England, some thirty years later after Maxwell's work (1897), J. J. Thompson used Braun's cathode ray tube, invented by German Karl Braun in 1897, to show that cathode rays were negatively charged. The tube operated by accelerating cathode emissions through an anode to strike a photoactive surface or screen. Thompson recognized the negatively charged particles in the rays. The name *electron* for the particles came from G. J. Stoney in 1891, denoting the unit of charge in experiments that passed electric currents through various chemicals. Thompson suggested a new atom, the "plum pudding" model, where the negative particles represented "raisins" and the "dough" contained the positive charge. He later referred to the particles as (Stoney's) electrons.

The atom's perceived structure was changing rapidly. In 1911, fourteen years later, Ernest Rutherford, who had Thompson as his mentor, showed Thompson's plum-pudding structure was incorrect. Rutherford, with help from Marsden and Geiger, used helium nuclei, positively charged alpha particles, to bombard very thin gold foil and record the flow passing through the foil as spectra on a fluorescent screen. The results were amazing. Most of the particles passed through the foil unaffected, as was expected. But some were deflected at an angle, and some rebounded straight back. Rutherford concluded that the atom was comprised of a very small, dense, positively charged nucleus at the atom's center with a cloud of negatively charged electrons surrounding it. The new nuclear model was now the face of the atom.

After Maxwell showed that light was an electromagnetic wave, prevailing thinkers felt that *any* wave was an undulation of a medium that carried it and that the light wave in space must move through a medium they termed the *ether*, which formed an absolute reference frame relative to the universe. Maxwell published his equations in 1860, but it took twenty years for them to be accepted by the scientific community. During this period, the ether's existence was discussed, but it wasn't until 1887 when two researchers at Western Reserve University in Cleveland, Ohio, decided to use an experiment to prove or disprove the ether's existence. The interference experiment Albert Michelson and Edward Morley conducted is only peripheral to the development of knowledge of atomic structure but still important.

Briefly, they used a light source, a half-coated glass plate, mirrors, and a telescope. If there was an ether, the interferometer experiment was set up to have the light travel sometimes in the direction of the ether and sometimes against it. The light beams would set up interference fringes when they were recombined, showing they had moved at different velocities through the ether. No such fringes were ever detected even though the experiment was conducted at opposite and other positions of the earth in its yearly motion around the sun. So there was no such thing as the ether and its absolute reference frame. The velocity of light appeared to be always measured the same. It was constant.

It has been said that Einstein did not know of this result in 1887. He, however, did publish the results of this experiment in a 1905 paper, the same year he published his special relativity theory. In this Michelson-Morley paper, he concluded that "without ether there is no special frame of reference against which different observers can measure this motion." Einstein also produced two postulates: (1) "the laws of physics are the same in all inertial reference frames" and (2) "the speed of light is the same in all inertial reference frames." We shall return repeatedly to these two postulates. An inertial reference frame is one in which the observers are not subject to an accelerating force.

In 1911, Niels Bohr, a Danish physicist, had observed previous work by Rydberg (1890) and Ritz in the study of emission spectra from various elements, using initially Geisler tubes, which were not unlike modern fluorescent tubes but able to use various emitting source elements within the tubes. Working with hydrogen, a single central nuclear proton with an orbiting electron, Ritz was able to produce a formula for emission lines in the infrared. Two of the lines were confirmed by Paschen in 1909. Bohr could see that these beautiful regular lines must be the result of an internal regularity in the electron field of the hydrogen atom. Studying the regularity, he was able to trace the source to three standard orbits in hydrogen that could produce these lines. With regard to the theoretical explanation of these lines and resulting orbits, he said in 1922, "Not one of the theories so far proposed appears to offer a satisfactory or even plausible way of explaining the laws of the line spectra."

The decade of the twenties was an extraordinarily fruitful period in attacking this enigma. Louis-Victor de Broglie was a French physicist who, in his 1924 doctoral thesis, postulated that the electron had a wave nature and that all matter had wave properties. His work showed that the wavelength of the electron's wave was an inverse function of its momentum, its mass-velocity product through Planck's constant, a proportionality constant, or

$$\lambda = \frac{h}{mv}$$

Three years later, Clinton Davisson and Lester Germer confirmed de Broglie's postulate by constructing a collimating device that directed an electron beam at a nickel crystal. The levels of atoms in the crystal diffracted the electrons and showed an intensity peak, and with that, an emission spectrum could be developed. Davisson and Germer were then able to show that the resulting calculated wavelength exactly matched de Broglie's equation.

De Broglie applied his equation to the Bohr model of the hydrogen electron. All three of Bohr's standard orbits had a circumference that were integral multiples of the wavelength from his wave equation. In simpler terms, all ends of the wave are connected with no overlap. De Broglie later gave the reason that the orbital waves must be integrally connected because of the necessity to maintain the wave-particle dual nature of matter.

It was at this point in the early twentieth century when events took a historic veer in a new direction with regard to atomic structure. Although Bohr's model of the hydrogen atom with coupled orbits was accepted, when the model was applied to heavier atoms, the interelectronic forces calculated did not agree with classical theory, and a new conundrum was encountered.

An alternative was offered in 1926 by Erwin Schrödinger, an Austrian theoretical physicist. Schrödinger put together the Bohr wave-behavior equations with the de Broglie equation to develop a mathematical model for the electron distribution in the atom. Rather than locating the electron exactly in its orbital, the Schrödinger model describes the *probability* that an electron can be located in a given region in a given time. This represented a true dichotomy for the understanding of the electron field part of atomic structure. Schrödinger never denied the existence of the electron itself, only that the probability model used an approximation of its location. The continuing development of quantum mechanics incorporating the Schrödinger model of the orbital electron was a point of no return for science. This was a watershed moment in which for the first time, science gave up the opportunity to understand the fine details of the atom's electron field for the foreseeable future. This was a commitment to pragmatics. Quantum mechanics is an elegant, beautifully constructed mathematical edifice that works. It works because we live in a statistical world. To illustrate, a common cup of coffee can contain in excess of 10^{23} atoms. That's a one followed by twenty-three zeros.

The period after the 1920s could be called the century of the accelerators. Modern quantum-theory associates fundamental forces with particles. By firing high-energy particles (e.g., protons) at the nucleus, the result is an impact and emission of other particles from the nucleus. It is the patterns of these scattered particles that researchers study. Holes and irregularities in the pattern allow prediction of new particles or corrections to previous work and to add descriptive equations where possible. It also allows them to build new proposed nuclear models. Two of the more significant models of this period were the liquid-drop model and the shell model. Much work was done with these two and were the precursors to the standard model of today. This model was initiated in the 1970s with the experimental confirmation (inferred) of the existence of quarks. Quarks, three each, are proposed to comprise the proton and neutron but, because of instability, are never seen alone. They were discovered by inference from their breakdown emission spectra. The reader should understand that the standard model is not a single physical entity but a body of knowledge or information, though it does, to a degree, suggest a physical model or models of the nucleus primarily, and the electron field.

The standard model theory describes the three fundamental forces: the electromagnetic force; the weak force, which includes the orbital electron; and the strong force, which includes the quarks. The fourth force is not included in the list because the model has no acceptable description of it—gravity or the associated dark force (e.g., dark-matter particles).

The Higgs boson is perhaps the current centerpiece of the standard model and expected by some to have a connection to gravity. The Higgs boson is ascribed to giving mass to all particles through its accompanying Higgs field. Its existence was predicted by physicist Peter Higgs in the 1960s and discovered at the Large Hadron Collider of CERN in 2012. Higgs himself thought it had no connection to gravity. The arguments both ways are ongoing. The context here, since the Higgs field is open and no coupled wave is involved, is that there is no evident connection.

Coupled Matter Wave

At this point, we are ready to focus on completing the finer detail of the picture by concentrating on the coupled matter wave through intuitive logic. Consideration of the orbital electron in an atom is to attempt to see something so "small" it is effectively out of sight. We have an option that some would argue with but I believe to be a realistic option. The Michelson-Morley experiment, if you remember, disallowed in nature any absolute space. Implicit in this is the exclusion of an absolute *scale*. Something can be "bigger" or smaller than something else, but there cannot be the largest or the smallest. So the idea, for example, that there can be a *different* system of natural laws for something or some region that is extremely small because it is extremely small (from our external viewpoint) is an idea excluded by nature. Therefore, we will "look closely" at the electron in coupled orbit by putting an observer (our mind's eye) next to it.

The two key ideas *The Absent Atom* is based on, as explained before, are the following: (1) that the orbital electron in coupled orbit must be moving along a local geodesic (a geodesic is a local length minimizing curve that an unaccelerated particle would follow) and (2) that geometric principles dictate that a hyperbolic or negative distortion of the space-time manifold must exist inside the atom. The *only* possibility for that hyperbolic distortion is the coupled matter wave in the electron field. These conclusions are the result of logic, but how can you show physical indication of the conclusions? The age-old methodology for that is to, again, put our mind's eye there.

To this point, we have covered several technical areas that are key to the model here and directed toward the more average reader. We have discussed multiply distorted two-spaces and explained how the entire manifold expresses and reflects the curvature of the individual identical group of distortions. In other words, a manifold with similar multiple positive curve distortions will ultimately reflect that curvature in the curvature of the entire manifold as positive (fig. 4). Conversely, a multiply distorted manifold with negative curvature distortions will result in a negative or hyperbolic manifold, a probable example of our own universe (fig. 5). We have also looked at the mathematical expression of curvature itself in its simpler form. This is Gaussian curvature, which is the product of the two reciprocals of the radii of curvature of a two-space (fig. 2). The radius is understood to be the magnitude value of a vector from the point on the surface to the center of radius of an arc segment on the surface, briefly.

It was an attempt to make clear to the reader that the radii of curvature of a negative surface are opposed in direction, with one radius having the opposite sign of the other, producing necessarily a negative or hyperbolic curvature to the surface at the selected point. Since lower-dimension geometries can be projected basically, in part, to higher ones, we can apply the idea to four-spaces such as our own gravitational field, an event matrix.

The idea of time dilation and length reduction in gravitational fields is sourced in the theory of general relativity. If a clock runs more slowly in a strong positive gravitational field and the more so the stronger the field, then the clock itself is a measure of the curvature of that gravitational field. The same applies to the reduction in length of a meterstick as a measure of curvature. There is no fundamental difference between the two radii of curvature in a two-space and the clock and meterstick of the positive gravitational field in determining the curvature of the field itself at a particular point. A basic premise of this model of atomic structure is that a hyperbolic or negative space exists within the volume of the atom that reflects a positive relaxation field externally (e.g., our gravitational field). That was demonstrated through the fundamental geometry presented here. A hyperbolic field is characterized by a reversal of the sign of one of the coordinates, either temporal or the spatial coordinate group. If a clock runs more slowly in a positive field, it will run *faster* in a negative field to reflect the reversal. Time, a clock, cannot run backward. Nature excludes it. The more important point may be that the coordinates are opposed.

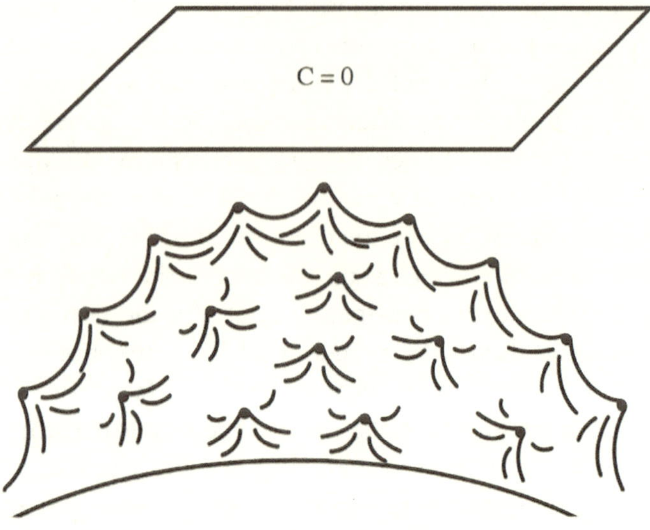

Uniformly distorted C = 0 manifold by spherical projections

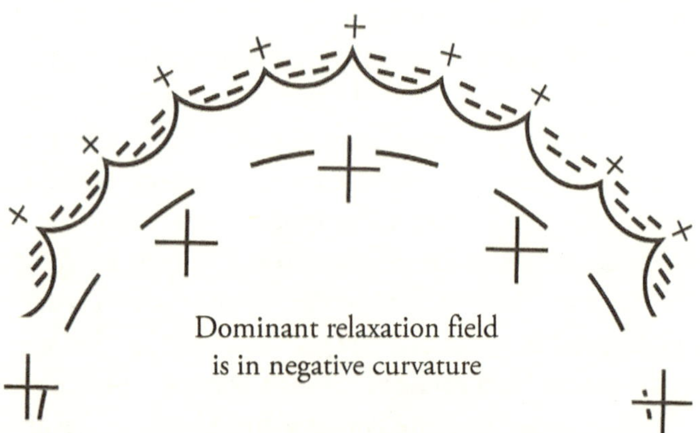

Overall manifold has positive curvature.
Large-dotted curved line

Fig. 4. The image above is intended to illustrate that the
uniform point distortion of a manifold will result in the overall
curvature of the manifold taking the curvature of the distortion.
Here is an example of an initially zero curvature plane being
positively curved by uniform positive point distortions.

$$C = k \frac{1}{R_1} \frac{1}{R_2} = k \frac{1}{R_1} \frac{1}{\infty} = 0$$

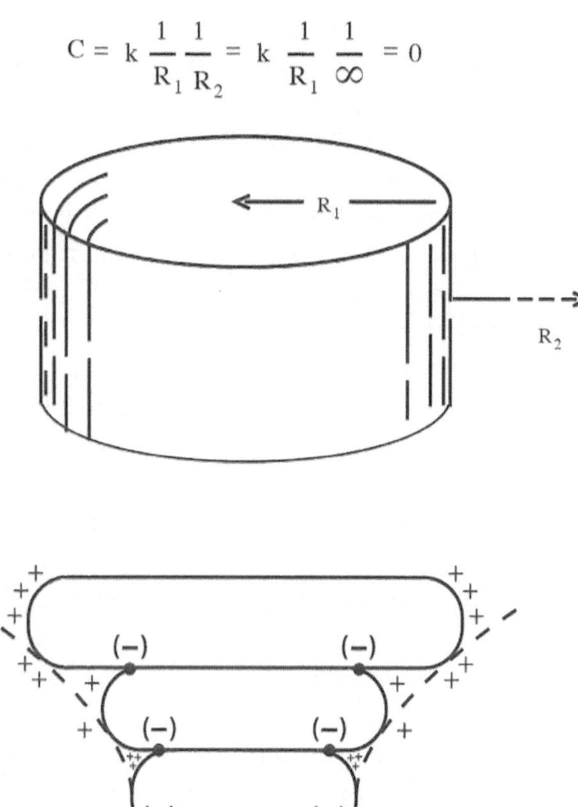

Fig. 5. This is an example of a negatively curved manifold, akin in the concept presented here to our own universe. It is a surface of zero curvature, here a cylinder, with the distortions caused by a sequence of compressing O-rings, producing a closed saddle surface. Although again the dominant surface area is positive, but the negative distortions result in a negative curvature of the entire manifold.

With the understanding that to be consistent with our initial assumption of a hyperbolic space, we are now ready to look at the electron from its own point of view or by putting our mind's eye observer next to it. At the scale of the electron from our external perspective, the electron's clock is running quite fast because it is in a negative closed space with a reversed time coordinate.

Again from an external point of view, to be consistent with a hyperbolic space, it (1) must be compressed and (2) have a high clock rate. By compressed we mean a metric (meterstick) would be reduced in length or shortened if taken into that space. As the field around and including the electron becomes smaller, its matter wave (de Broglie wave) recedes. The electron matter wave recedes because the complete coupled wave cannot become part of the compressed field. Thus, the relative view the electron has in this process is that its de Broglie wavelength has lengthened. Locally it approaches an inertial reference frame condition and moves along a geodesic. And for that reason, it radiates no electromagnetic wave.

Further, since we have presented this system as a two-space, its reality from our outside perspective is that of a three-space. The coupled wave is spread along an elliptical surface. The closed hyperbolic space can be thought of from our perspective as an elliptical shell.

What does the above give us? We have the electron circling the nucleus, from an external perspective, in a closed negative space. Externally, it is curving in an electrostatic field, so it seemingly should radiate electromagnetic energy. But in the closed negative space, it is moving *locally* along a straight line, or geodesic. It is in an inertial reference frame.

Remember Leucippus! Since the electron obeys Newton's laws of mechanics, locally it is stable and does not radiate electromagnetic energy. Every other electron in an atom heavier than hydrogen in stable orbit is in a different reference frame. So here, interelectronic forces cannot obey classical analytical treatment in the context of our continuous field model. This has been determined in the lab. These forces must be described by translation equations across reference frames (Einstein's field equations).

When the electron becomes in phase with its matter wave field, the full field coalesces into a single coupled wave, bringing energy from the field into the single coupled wave. I believe we can speculate that this energy must go somewhere, and it is logical to think that this energy ends up in the negative space-time curved around the electron. *Space-time itself has collapsed around the electron's orbit.* It is difficult to say, but there may also be other energy here, as in potential energy, from the electrostatic field. From the perspective of the electron, since it experiences long periods passing in a single electron orbit, it must see its world as *getting larger* and its matter wave receding into the distance, conserving the de Broglie relation consistent with a local inertial reference frame, and sees the uniqueness of the complete coupled matter wave as an unchangeable entity alone since it *cannot collapse* with the negative field. This suggests the invariance of a universal constant in that the coupled wave looks the same from different reference frames. The collapse is hyperbolic from an external perspective since the electron's clock is running fast, again a reversal of the time coordinate. Further, the reader should understand that the event sequence above is intended to elaborate on a causal connection. The changes described above would happen instantly in nature.

For you, the reader, to have a better grasp of the conditions around the coupled orbital electron, place yourself as moving in a long hallway where the interior, including yourself, is collapsing in size and your clock is running faster. Further the hallway (walls, floor, and ceiling) cannot collapse; it is *invariant* in size. What do you see? You will see the hallway getting larger and longer, the walls receding, and the hallway lengthening in front of you. You cannot see *yourself* as getting smaller because your immediate surroundings are getting smaller at the same rate. You can extend the idea above to the electron in coupled orbit as it sees its matter wave stretch out and the electron moves into a space that is an inertial reference frame, obeying Newton's laws and Euclid's geometry. Since locally it is not accelerating, the electron cannot radiate electromagnetic energy.

To summarize the above, we have made some basic assumptions and following observations:

(1) The electron in coupled orbit moves in an inertial reference frame. This is sourced in the understanding from Michelson-Morley that an absolute reference frame cannot exist and in the understanding that the radiation of EM energy by a charged particle under acceleration is fundamental. If it is not radiating, it is either static or moving in an inertial reference frame.

(2) Elementary geometry dictates that a uniformly distorted continuous manifold will assume the curvature of the distortion (fig. 4).

(3) A distortion of a continuous manifold will have a surrounding relaxation field of opposite curvature to the distortion (figs. 4 and 5).

(4) In a positive manifold, formal characteristic curvatures will have the radii of the same mathematical sign. In a negative manifold, such curvature will be opposed or have opposed mathematical signs.

(5) In a four-space such as the space-time manifold, the characteristic radii of a two-space are equivalent to the temporal and spatial coordinates of the event field (four-space). The spatial coordinates will have distance values (e.g., meters), and the temporal coordinates will have clock metrics (seconds).

(6) Principles of geometry can be projected from lower non-complex dimensions to higher more complex dimensions. For example, from a two-space to a four-space.

The fact that the coupled electron follows an inertial reference frame means that the reference frame extends over the entire coupled orbit of the electron. It also means that the space is curved and closed. This *must* be a hyperbolic space from the most basic geometric principles.

In such a hyperbolic space, the electron's coordinates are opposed. With a fast rather than slow-running clock and compressed spatial coordinates, a coupled matter wave that is (equivalently) locked, the electron must *experience* an expanded space to be in an inertial reference frame. The coupled electron cannot experience a change in its own clock rate. If the space compresses but the locked matter wave *does not*, the electron will experience the matter wave as far extended, and de Broglie's relation holds locally. As outside observers, we see a closed, compressed space and a fast-running clock, again opposed coordinates but the opposite ones, and still a hyperbolic space.

External Perspective	Electron Perspective
• Compressed space around coupled matter wave • Fast-running clock for electron • Temporal coordinate reversed • Hyperbolic space	• Extended space • Long wavelength, obeys de Broglie's relation and Newton's and Euclid's laws • Moving along a geodesic

It is remarkable that while the same space around the coupled matter wave is seen from our external perspective as a *compressed* hyperbolic space, the electron sees in reality that compressed space as an *expanded* space. Both perspectives experience a fast-running clock, although the electron would only "see" a normal clock. The equivalent of our years could pass for the electron in a single orbit, but that would be fractions of a picosecond for us. Both perspectives are in a compressed space though the electron interprets it as an expanded space because the complete coupled wave cannot collapse since that would change its position in space, for one reason. It is also remarkable here as the complete coupled wave appears to be a *physical invariant*. Since the electron is moving along a local geodesic, it is implicit that it moves in a closed space extending completely around the nucleus.

A side but significant question remains that doesn't affect this model. When the electron's matter wave coalesces into coupling, why does it stabilize there? Could the answer possibly be something as prosaic as the wave field energy accumulating to some critical point that nature must put it into distorting the space-time manifold negatively? Or could the answer be a mirroring of the coupled wave with the entire universe, apparent only from some higher arcane reference frame, knowledge buried in the future?

The Nucleus

The nucleus in this continuous field model must be a continuation of the electron field structure. It must be a continuous field dominated completely by the coupled matter wave. The nucleons, the proton and the neutron, are connected by the strong force, which here is likely a purely gravitational force. This is a positive gravitational field acting across an inflection region between the nucleons and reacting with a negative gravitational field. The compressed space around a coupled matter wave in the nucleus means that the interacting forces will be of very short range. This would complicate any laboratory efforts to duplicate the coupled wave in the nucleus or the electron field because of the exquisite accuracies and precision that would likely be required.

So we are now dealing with both the nuclear proton and the nuclear neutron having a coupled matter wave structure. Our current knowledge of the nucleus is so limited that at one time, there have been as many as twenty-plus formally presented models of the nucleus. Proposing any kind of nuclear structure without a detailed, verifiable, at least visualizable, form is hazardous at best.

The electron field of a typical atom may be hundreds of nuclear diameters away from the nucleus itself. So you can assume that any nuclear coupled matter wave is going to be of very high energy. A conceivable but highly speculative example may be the interaction of a positron and an electron, which usually results in mutual annihilation of their respective masses into pure energy. The interaction can also enable a few unstable states, called positronium, that eventually annihilate. Suppose, however, that every now and then, but rarely, the result is a binary couplet that is stable, electrically neutral, and of very high energy. There is a great disparity between the rest masses of the electron and positron and a nucleon such as a proton or neutron—the neutron having a mass order of magnitudes greater. But if that great interaction energy can be converted to mass, that disparity in rest masses can go away. Again, this is highly speculative but is the type of thinking I believe is required to achieve a successful continuous field nucleus. More realistically, there is no doubt that continuous field models of the nucleus will surface in the future. In our nod to the particle theorists, perhaps we will eventually see a quark with such a structure.

The Hyperbolic Universe

Go back and look at figs. 4 and 5. See how the *entire* manifold takes the curvature of the imposed local curvature. Not surprising, right? So it should not be surprising that if the fundamental distortion of the space-time manifold is negative or hyperbolic, then our universe itself *should also be hyperbolic*. The early physicists were excellent geometrists, and it was straightforward to them. They publicly stated that the universe was probably hyperbolic. Yet many of the present scientific community think our universe is fully positively curved and that total gravitational collapse is possible. I believe that such thinking will change.

Dark Energy

Dark energy, in brief, is the observation that the galaxies are all moving away from one another, not only moving but also accelerating away. Where does the force come from to generate such acceleration? Our answer is the simplest one. The coupled matter wave structure of all matter produces negative or hyperbolic curvature. The natural motion of galaxies in a hyperbolic universe is accelerated separation from each other. Take two test points on a hyperbolic surface and moving initially in parallel. They will move away from each other at an *increasing* rate. This is a basic principle that can be projected from a three-space that we can visualize to the four-space space-time manifold. As such, dark energy as a mystery goes away.

Since we do not experience negative fields and their attendant fast-running clocks in our everyday experience, the average individual may question their existence. The problem is, of course, that they exist only in "inaccessible" places, such as inside the atom and in intergalactic space. Perhaps there is some implicit evidence in interstellar space, but that would have to await possible future space probes.

Black Holes

The budding physicist usually first encounters the term *singularity* in the study of complex functions. These functions of a complex variable involve a pseudo-four-space called the complex plane. Here, there are bounded closed regions where descriptive equations break down by exhibiting numbers divided by zeros or infinities. The accepted understanding is that these closed regions, called singularities, represent a breakdown in theory and do not have a separate reality. The analogy extends in our universe to what are known as black holes. Some consider them as physical singularities representing a breakdown in gravitational theory and, like the singularities of the complex plane, do not have a separate physical reality. Others, probably the majority, disagree.

In what is considered total gravitational collapse, matter falls together in a star to the point and beyond that its gravitational field maximum, which is always at the gravitating body's surface, has an orbital velocity equal to the velocity of light. Thus, no light can escape at the star's radius, and a "black hole" is created. That radius of the star when light can no longer escape is called the Schwarzschild radius. The reader should understand that the Schwarzschild radius has no separate reality but is a solution to Einstein's general relativity differential equations and ostensibly depends on total gravitational collapse. The neutron star has the highest density of any known star. In it, the neutrons are packed closely together, approaching the density of the atom's nucleus. Some studies have shown that the orbital velocity at the surface of a neutron star is significantly less than light velocity. This is more evidence that a black hole has a questionable existence.

In the coupled matter wave model presented here, the universe's fundamental gravitational force is reactive or repelling, meaning, total gravitational collapse is impossible, so to the extent that total gravitational collapse is necessary for a black hole to exist, black holes do not have a physical reality.

Empirical Possibilities

Since absolute spaces do not exist and "small" or "large" have no absolute meaning, the coupled matter wave should be reproducible in a laboratory with an appropriately designed accelerator. Once obtained, it should exhibit all the characteristics this continuous field model has described. The engineering applications would be manifold.

Continuous Field and Particle Theories

Here we are describing a continuous field model of the atom. We live in a world of perceived particles, and most atomic models presented by the scientific community are based on particle theory. Our system of logic itself, our mathematics, is grounded on the idea that a physical point exists, ergo a closed bounded region of infinitesimal diameter. But reality, I believe, is that we live in a universe that is a continuous field that excludes physical points. Our accepted logic system works because it doesn't need to extend down to the scale of the atom where an influence could appear. Einstein said it best:

> The physical reality of space is represented by a field whose components are continuous functions of four independent variables—the coordinates of space and time. Since the theory of general relativity implies the representation of physical reality by a continuous field, the concept of particles or material points cannot play a fundamental part nor can the concept of motion. The particle can only appear as a limited region in space in which the field strength or the energy density are particularly high.[1]

Mother Nature cleverly stores energy in fields as distortions of those fields. In a canoe, we watch our paddle make eddies and swirls

---

[1] Albert Einstein, *Ideas and Opinions* (Crown Publishing, 1954), 348.

in the water that move and bounce against the boat and each other, occasionally merging to create a larger eddy. Water is an example of a fluid, as is the gas in our atmosphere. We see eddies popping off the trailing edge of a stalling aircraft wing. We see eddies in the atmosphere gas as dust devils, tornadoes, cyclones, and hurricanes. We see them in the Great Red Spot on Jupiter and in the "fluid" atmosphere of the Sun. They have one dominant thing in common: they are part of a continuous field. If we could run a line through the eddy in the water, it would follow the spins and whirls but would ultimately come out of the other side unbroken. The eddy, too, is part of a continuous field. Energy is stored in all these vortices. Can it be surprising that nature stores energy in our ultimate conscious field, the space-time manifold, as a vortex, the coupled matter wave?

Bibliography

Bohr, Niels. *The Theory of Spectra and Atomic Constitution.* Alpha Editions, 2020.

Davies, P. C. W., and J. R. Brown. *The Ghost in the Atom.* Cambridge University Press, 1986.

Einstein, Albert. *Ideas and Opinions.* Crown Publishers, 1985.

———. *The Life and Times.* Avon Books, 1971.

———. *The Meaning of Relativity.* Princeton University Press, 1953.

———. *Out of My Later Years.* Citadel Press, 1956.

Ellis, George F. R., and Ruth M. Williams. *Flat and Curved Space-Times.* Clarendon Press, 1988.

Fleisch, Daniel. *Maxwell's Equations.* Cambridge University Press, 2013.

Greene, Brian. *The Hidden Reality.* Random House, 2011.

Kaku, Michio. *Hyperspace.* Oxford University Press, 1994.

Kaku, Michio, and Jennifer Trainer. *Beyond Einstein.* Bantam Books, 1987.

Lindley, David. *The Dream Universe.* Doubleday, 2020.

Liberies, Amo. *Introduction to Molecular Orbital Theory.* Holt Rinehart and Winston Inc., 1966.

Misner, Charles W., Kip S. Thorne, and J. A. Wheeler. *Gravitation.* W. H. Freeman and Co., 1973.

Musser, George. *String Theory.* Penguin Group, 2008.

Pagels, Heinz R. *Perfect Symmetry.* Bantam Books, 1991.

Schwinger, Julian. *Einstein's Legacy.* Scientific American Books, 1986.

Smolin, Lee. *The Trouble with Physics.* Houghton Mifflin, 2007.

———. *Einstein's Unfinished Revolution.* Penguin Books, 2020.

Taylor, Edwin F., and John A. Wheeler. *Spacetime Physics.* 2nd ed. W. H. Freeman and Co., 1992.

Thorne, Kip S. *Black Holes and Time Warps*. W. W. Norton and Co., 1994.

Wald, Robert M. *General Relativity*. University of Chicago Press, 1984.

About the Author

After his BS, William Reveley joined NASA and began performing research and development in the area of advanced spacecraft environmental control systems.

In continuing R & D, he supported the Apollo moon landing program and carried out structural analysis for the Spacelab project. In the space shuttle program, he was a member of the source evaluation board and was later a payload mission manager. As a team member of the International Space Station program, he was deputy manager of the systems and elements analysis office. At agency headquarters, his responsibilities included the position of technical manager of small launch vehicle development.

His postgrad work dealt primarily with mathematics and physics. He has received several individual performance and team awards and is currently retired and living with his family in North Carolina.

www.ingramcontent.com/pod-product-compliance
Lightning Source LLC
Chambersburg PA
CBHW022123150726
47990CB00003B/1487